W9-DBM-496

This Book Belongs To

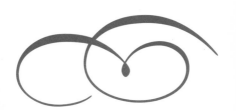

The Story of Christmas

The
Story
of
Christmas

Jennifer Greenway

Ariel Books

Andrews and McMeel
Kansas City

Frontispiece: Gustav Doré, THE NATIVITY, 1860's.

ISBN: 0-8362-3088-4

Library of Congress Catalog Card Number: 94-72161

Contents

The Angel Gabriel's Message

$\mathcal{O}$nce long ago there lived a young woman named Mary in the village of Nazareth high in the mountains above the sea of Galilee. At the time when Mary lived, the people of Palestine, who were known as the Jews or the Israelites, were part of the Roman Empire, and their king, whose name was Herod, was under Roman rule. Although Herod was king of the

Jews, he had no love for his people. Instead, he allowed them to be mistreated and enslaved by the Romans. The people of Israel longed to be free, and their prophets often spoke of the day when a savior would be born among them.

Mary of Nazareth was beautiful, good, and pure of heart, and everyone who knew her loved her. One day as Mary was praying alone in her room for the people of Israel, a brilliant golden light came streaming through the window. "Hail Mary full of grace," a lovely voice called out to her, "the Lord is with you, for you are blessed among women!" And the archangel Gabriel appeared before her. He was dressed in cloth of dazzling snow-white, and his face was radiant as the morning sun. Mary was frightened and fell to her knees. But the angel comforted her.

"Fear not, Mary," he said gently, "for you have found favor with God. Listen to the news I bring you! Behold, you shall soon bear a child, a son, and you shall call him

Jesus. He will be great beyond all other men, for he shall be the Son of God the Father, the highest of the high. And the Lord God will give him the throne of his father David, and he shall reign over the people of Israel forever, and his kingdom will be without end, but shall last forever."

After the angel Gabriel had given Mary this message, he vanished. But what he had prophesied soon came to pass. Although Mary was a virgin, she soon found herself with child.

The Story of Christmas

Mary was betrothed to a carpenter of Nazareth named Joseph. So she told Joseph of the angel Gabriel's visit, and confided in him that she was to bear a child who would be the savior of Israel and the true Son of God. At first, Joseph was troubled by Mary's story, but that night a wonderful dream came to him. In the dream, a voice, more commanding and more beautiful than any he had ever heard before, called down to him from the sky: "Joseph, son of David, listen to my words. Fear no evil and doubt nothing. But take Mary of Nazareth as your bride, for the child she carries is conceived of the Holy Ghost and is the son of God the Father. And he shall be called Jesus, the Messiah, for he shall save his people from sin."

When Joseph awoke from his dream he gazed up at the night sky, and at the bright stars. His heart was at peace, for he knew that he, too, had heard the voice of the angel Gabriel, and that Mary's child was the Son of God and the savior the

15

people of Israel had so long awaited. And so Joseph kneeled down and thanked God for his goodness, and as Gabriel had commanded, he took Mary for his bride.

The Angel Gabriel's Message

The Birth of Baby Jesus

After their wedding, Mary and Joseph settled in Joseph's small house in Nazareth. They lived there together in great happiness and waited for the birth of the baby Jesus. But as the time for the birth of Mary's child drew near, a Roman soldier came riding into Nazareth. He stopped in the market square and read out a proclamation from Augustus Caesar, Emperor of

The Birth of Baby Jesus

Rome. In the proclamation Augustus Caesar declared that all the world should be taxed. To pay this tax each man must go to the city his family had originally come from. Now, Joseph was descended from King David of old. King David's city was the town of Bethlehem, far away in the mountains of Moab in the state of Judea. Therefore, Joseph and Mary must travel at once to Bethlehem.

❋ Mary and Joseph's friends and neighbors were horrified. The journey to

The Story of Christmas

Bethlehem was long and difficult, especially in wintertime. It took a strong man traveling alone four days to reach Bethlehem on foot. How could Joseph take Mary on such a hard journey when she was so close to bearing a child? But Mary was not afraid. She was sure that God would take care of her. She also knew that according to the great Hebrew prophet Micah the savior of the people of Israel was to be born in the town of Bethlehem. And so she gladly prepared for the journey.

The Birth of Baby Jesus

✤ With Joseph's help, Mary loaded their small gray donkey with provisions for the journey. She packed skins of water and loaves of bread and dried fruit and nuts. She also packed blankets, and clothes for the baby, for she knew that her son would surely be born on the journey. Then she and Joseph set out on the steep path to Bethlehem.

✤ The road Mary and Joseph followed was bare and rocky. It climbed over the hills that bordered Nazareth, then dipped down across the broad plain of Esdraelon. Wheat and millet grew there in the spring and summer, but it was winter, and the fields were freshly plowed. The dull brown color of the earth was discouraging, as was the rain that fell there ceaselessly in the winter months. However, before long, the path began climbing again.

❋ Soon Mary and Joseph were winding their way through the mountains of Samaria. Now there were terraces of olive and fig trees on either side of them. As they rose higher, they climbed out of the clouds and into the sunlight. It was pleasant to travel in the bright sunshine for a change, but the wind from the mountaintops was bitterly cold. Mary wrapped her cloak ever more tightly around her to stay warm. She rode on the little gray donkey, while Joseph walked alongside her.

❋ In the daytime the weather in the mountains was not too bad, but at night the temperatures quickly dropped below freezing. Mary and Joseph took shelter where they could. Sometimes they slept under large oak and sycamore trees. Sometimes they slept in the camps of shepherds. However, they did not stop in any of the villages along the way, for they were in a hurry to reach Bethlehem in time to pay their taxes, and more urgently, in time for the birth of Mary's child. Up and down they went until at last they reached the state of Judea. Judea was famous for its vineyards. In the summer months the hills of Judea were green and fair, and rang with the cries of the

The Birth of Baby Jesus

workers busy tending the plump grapes. But at this time of year, the vines were dry and leafless and the hills were silent and empty.

❊ Mary was growing weary now, and Joseph could see that the time when her child would be born was approaching. He knew that the small gray donkey could not go much faster. Still, Joseph urged the creature to speed up its pace, for he was eager to reach Bethlehem, and find a place where they might rest. He and Mary passed hastily through the great city of

The Story of Christmas

Jerusalem, and continued on along the small winding road that led to Bethlehem.

❋ Darkness was falling, and the air was growing cold when Joseph and Mary at last reached Bethlehem. As was the custom in Palestine, the town of Bethlehem was built on a hilltop. The two weary travelers gazed up at the lights of the town longingly. How warm and inviting they looked. Mary and Joseph's hearts lightened as they drew near the town gate. Yet when they got there, their spirits sank again. A great crowd was gathered around the gatekeeper, for men had traveled from far and wide to record their names in the census and pay Augustus Caesar his tax.

✿ Mary, in particular, was almost overcome with dismay. She could feel that the time had come for her child to be born. But the village of Bethlehem was so crowded she could not imagine how they would ever find a room for the night. However, she was careful not to show her distress, but smiled at Joseph encouragingly. Joseph, for his part, bravely led the small gray donkey past the gatekeeper and down Bethlehem's narrow streets.

❄ First, Mary and Joseph stopped at the village inn. But they found that every room had long ago been taken. From there, they went from house to house, begging a room for the night. However, everyone in Bethlehem who had a bed to spare had already given it to some traveler or other. Everywhere Mary and Joseph stopped the answer was the same: there was no shelter to be had.

The Birth of Baby Jesus

❋ Mary turned pale, for by this time she was tired and ill.

"What shall we do?" she whispered. Joseph did his best to comfort her. "Do not worry, Mary," he said softly. "God will take care of us. We shall soon find a place to rest." But as they were turned away from house after house, he, too, became anxious.

❋ It was growing very late. The sky was pitch dark. A bitter wind swept down from the hills above Bethlehem where the shepherds were busy guarding their flocks. The

The Story of Christmas

lights of the town were now slowly going out, one by one. The only light left came from the stars overhead, which twinkled as brightly as torches.

❄ "We must find a bed somewhere," Joseph said. He led Mary back to the inn where they had first stopped, and rang the bell. For some minutes there was no answer. The innkeeper and his family had already gone to bed. However, at last, the innkeeper opened the door crossly. "What do you want?"

❄ Joseph explained that he and his

wife had come all the way from Nazareth, and had been wandering the streets for hours, looking for a place to stay.

❖ The innkeeper was not impressed. "I have no room," he said. "You'd better get on your way." But then Joseph told him that Mary was about to have a child, and the innkeeper relented. "Very well," he said reluctantly. "As I told you, I have no rooms left, but if you wish, you may spend the night in the stable. It's warmer there than it is outdoors."

The Story of Christmas

❋ The innkeeper led Joseph and Mary, and the little gray donkey across a dark yard to a small limestone cave. The cave, which was level with the street, served as the inn's stables. Leaving them his lamp, the innkeeper then sleepily made his way back to his own warm bed.

❋ Joseph raised the lamp high while he and Mary looked around. The stable was a rough place. The floor was of hard-packed earth, scattered with straw, and the walls and roof were of rugged stone. The mouth of the cave had been blocked off with slats of wood. The gaps between the slats were so wide you could see out onto the dark street and the starry sky above. Yet for all its roughness, the stable offered protection and it was quiet and peaceful.

❋ A pair of huge oxen gazed wonderingly at Joseph and Mary, their round brown eyes gentle and solemn. An old ass hee-hawed gently in greeting, and the white horse in the corner slowly swished his tail to and fro. Even the little pink pig tied to a pole in the center of the cave appeared to welcome Joseph and Mary, nodding his plump head up and down at them.

✳ Mary was pleased to see that the straw in the stable was clearly fresh, for it had a good grass-like smell. "And there is a cradle we can lay the baby in when he's born," she said to Joseph, pointing at a large sturdy wooden manger in the corner, which was full of clean straw. Joseph nodded and, setting the lamp on the floor, laid out his cloak for Mary to lie down on. The lamp flared and went out, and there was no light but the golden glow of the stars.

❋ Wind whispered softly around the stable. The clouds blew this way and that across the vast night sky. In the hills above Bethlehem, the shepherds kept watch over their sleeping flocks, while high up on the mountaintops, snow drifted silently onto the quiet earth. And inside the stable, Mary gave birth to the baby Jesus.

The Story of Christmas

❉ As soon as Jesus was born, Mary wrapped him in clean swaddling clothes, and laid him gently in the manger. The baby Jesus kicked his legs in the air, and waved his hands, and smiled. There was a golden radiance about the child, like the radiance of the angel Gabriel's face, only a thousand times brighter. Every living creature in the stable felt it.

❉ The oxen stared at the baby. Then they slowly inched forward, lowering their great heads as they came. The old ass kneeled down right beside the manger and peered in at the child, breathing as quietly as he was able. The white horse in the corner pricked up his ears, and approached the manger with timid steps. Even the little pig in the center gnawed at his rope until it broke, so that he, too, could go over and pay his respects to the newborn child.

❖ The little gray donkey poked his head over the head of the manger. He gazed down on the baby Jesus with special pride, for it was he who had carried Mary all the way from her home in Nazareth to the town of Bethlehem.

❄ Even the wild creatures who made their homes in the stable came forward to look on the Christ child. Along came the rabbits who lived in a hole in the corner, the mice who lived beneath the grain buckets, and the sparrows who nested in the roof.

❄ As each of these creatures, tame and wild, approached the manger, the baby

The Birth of Baby Jesus

Jesus smiled, and nodded, and stretched out his arms, as if to welcome each and every one.

❈ Although the stable of Bethlehem was only a very humble place, that night, under the light of the moon and stars, it shone like a great golden palace. Indeed, that night, the simple stable was a palace—the most wonderful, splendid palace ever known—for it was there that the King of Kings was born, to lie in a manger full of straw.

The Shepherds of Bethlehem

As the tame and wild creatures of the stable came forward to pay their respects to the baby Jesus, the shepherds in the hills above Bethlehem began to call to one another in loud, excited voices. Up in the sky was a sight such as they had never seen before. There was a new star in the sky above Bethlehem. It was a star brighter and more beautiful than any the shepherds had ever seen. Its light shone down over the sleeping town more brightly than even the moon.

✦ The shepherds of Bethlehem, who watched the stars faithfully, wondered what the presence of this new star could mean. They called out to one another, and threw back their heads, and gazed up at the star in wonder. The star grew brighter, and seemed to draw closer and closer. Then, all at once, the shepherds saw that the star was not a star at all, but the angel Gabriel, standing before them in all his glory.

The Story of Christmas

❧ For a moment the shepherds were frightened. Some hid their eyes. Others fell to their knees in prayer. But the angel Gabriel comforted them.

❧ "Fear not, my good shepherds. Behold! I bring you tidings of great joy, which shall be for all people. Unto you in the town of Bethlehem a savior is born this day. His name is Jesus Christ the Lord. Let this be a sign to you: You shall find the baby Jesus wrapped in swaddling clothes, and lying in a manger."

The Shepherds of Bethlehem

❧ Then the angel faded from view. But across the hills of Bethlehem rang out a music the like of which had never been heard on Earth before. It was the heavenly host singing their joy. All the angels of heaven had gathered over the humble shepherds' heads to sing out in praise of the baby Jesus.

❧ "Glory be to God in the highest," the angels sang. "On Earth let there be peace and goodwill to all men, for the Son of God has been born this night in Bethlehem."

The Story of Christmas

There were trumpets and violins, and a music like the piping of flutes, but of a tone more silvery and fair than any flutes made by human hands. The humble shepherds fell to their knees and wept with joy, for the music was so beautiful it pierced their hearts, through and through.

When the last notes of the angels' song had faded from the hills, all became silent again. There was only the same bright star the shepherds had glimpsed earlier, shining above Bethlehem to mark the miraculous events of the night. And the boldest among the shepherds rose to their feet and said to one another, "Let us go down into Bethlehem, and see this miracle, the birth of the Son of God, which the Lord our Father has made known to us."

❧ So the shepherds took up their crooks and led their flocks out of the hills and down to Bethlehem. They did not know where the stable where Jesus was born lay, or how they would find the child in the manger. But they followed the star, which

49

moved before them as they came down into Bethlehem, lighting up their path as the rising sun lights up the edges of the world.

    ❧ Soon the shepherds' feet were crossing the dark yard of the Bethlehem inn. They timidly approached the entrance of the stable where Mary and Joseph were watching over the newborn baby Jesus. Mary and Joseph came to greet their visitors, and Mary asked them how they had come there. The shepherds told her what they had seen in the fields above Bethlehem. Mary listened to the shepherds' story with joy, and took the words they spoke into her heart, and long pondered them. The shepherds then asked to see the child, and Mary and Joseph gladly obliged.

❧ When the baby Jesus saw the shepherds and their flocks, he raised his arms toward them in welcome. The shepherds fell to their knees, with their sheep gathered close around them. After a moment the young lambs rose up and tottered toward the manger with uneven steps, while the baby Jesus reached out and petted their woolly heads with his tiny hands.

❧ Later, when the shepherds tried to describe what they had seen in the Christ child's face, they always found that their tongues would not shape words to tell what their hearts felt. But the memory of his look remained inside them, like a drop of water to quench their thirst, salt to season their food, or a fire to warm them in the cold.

❧ The shepherds stayed all night in the stable, keeping watch over baby Jesus and

The Shepherds of Bethlehem

Mary and Joseph. So it was that the King of Kings was first attended by a crowd of humble shepherds, and the shepherds of Bethlehem were the first to learn the news that the Son of God had been born, and a savior had come to Israel.

The Three Wise Men

The shepherds were not the only ones who saw the star of Bethlehem. Three other men had also seen the star. These three men were kings of the East. The first was Melchior, a king of Arabia, the second was Caspar, the king of Tharsis, a kingdom far to the North, and the third was Balthazar, the king of Ethiopia. These three kings were wise men and scholars, and

The Three Wise Men

were called by the name of Magi or men of knowledge.

The three Magi had spent many long years studying the path of the stars. When they first saw the new star in the sky they knew that it was a great omen. According to many ancient prophecies, the appearance of such a brilliant new star in the sky heralded the coming of the savior— he who was to be known as the King of the Jews, and the true Son of God. So the three wise men collected gifts for the new king. Then they joined together and traveled many long, hard miles until they reached the city of Jerusalem.

👑 When the three Magi arrived in Jerusalem, they asked everyone they met, "Where is the savior? Where is he that is born King of the Jews? We have seen his star in the East and have come to worship him."

👑 The people of Jerusalem were puzzled and amazed by the words of the three wise men. Soon news of their journey

The Three Wise Men

spread through the entire city, until King Herod heard about it. Now, as you know, Herod was the ruler of Israel at the time. But although Herod called himself King of the Jews he was not a real king to his people. Instead of protecting the people of Israel, Herod had given them over to be slaves of Rome.

At the news that a new king had been born, Herod's heart was filled with fear and hatred. However, Herod was careful to hide his true feelings from all around him. Instead, he called together his priests and counselors. He asked them where it was prophesied that he who was to be the Messiah, Son of God and King of the Jews, was to be born.

 ☄ "In the town of Bethlehem," came the reply, "for that is the prophecy of Micah who said, 'You Bethlehem, in the land of Judea, you are hardly the least among the princes of Judea, for out of you shall come a governor that shall rule the people of Israel!'"

The Three Wise Men

✦ After Herod heard these words, he brooded for some time. Then he called the three wise men to his palace and greeted them graciously. He questioned them diligently about when they had first seen the star. Each one replied the same. The star had appeared twelve days before. When Herod heard this, he knew that the savior the old prophecies had spoken of had surely been born. So he sent the three wise men speeding on their way to Bethlehem.

✦ "Go to Bethlehem," Herod told the

The Story of Christmas

wise men, pitching his voice low and sweet, "and search diligently for the young child. When you find him, bring him here to me in Jerusalem so that I may worship him also."

Herod convinced the three wise men that he meant well, and gave them many provisions to help them on their journey. But in his heart, Herod wished only to find the baby Jesus so that he might kill him before the boy could grow up and become the King of the Jews and the savior of his people.

The Three Wise Men

👑 The three wise men rode off, following the same narrow road to Bethlehem as Mary and Joseph had before them. They were a strange sight to behold. Unlike the other travelers on the road to Bethlehem, who went by foot or by donkey, the Magi rode along on tall camels draped with beautiful silks and tapestries. Before them, they carried the gifts they had brought for the baby Jesus, in caskets of rare wood and precious metals.

👑 They rode through the day and into

the night. As soon as darkness fell, the three wise men knew that they were following the right path, for the star they had first seen far off in the East shone before them, lighting their way with a calm and steady radiance.

The three wise men followed the star past the gates of Bethlehem, and down the quiet streets until they reached the stable behind the inn. Joseph, Mary, and the baby Jesus were inside. Joseph and Mary were dazzled by the splendor of their latest visitors. But the three Magi kneeled down before the baby Jesus on the rough stable floor, and gave him the gifts they had carried for so many miles.

Melchior of Arabia brought the baby Jesus a casket of gold. The gift of gold symbolized the wealth of humankind—the talents and health and strength of all the peoples of the earth. Balthazar of Ethiopia brought a casket of frankincense for the holy child. This fragrant resin was burned during sacred ceremonies in his country, and symbolized the spirit of humankind and the prayers of the people of the world. Caspar of Tharsis brought myrrh. This pungent spice was used by his people to soothe burns and wounds of all kinds, and was given to the Christ child as a symbol of how he would, by his life and death, heal the ills of humankind. After the Magi had presented their gifts to the baby Jesus, he raised his head to them and smiled. It seemed to them that the light of the star was in his eyes, and that his smile had gone into their hearts and would stay there always. And the three wise men, the three kings of the East, bowed to Mary and Joseph and departed.

❦ However, the Magi did not go back to Jerusalem as Herod had instructed them. In a dream, the voice of the angel Gabriel had warned them to beware of Herod. So instead, the three wise kings rode their camels over the hills on the far side of Bethlehem. Then the three followed another path back to their homes, bearing the glad news of the birth of the Lord Jesus, the Son of God, with them.

The Flight from Herod

*T*he three wise men had managed to escape Herod's clutches. But Joseph and Mary and the baby Jesus were not out of danger yet. Herod waited for the wise men to return, but it was not long before he learned that they had departed by another path, and were never coming back to Jerusalem. When Herod heard this his fury was boundless. Now he was sure that the child he feared, the child who was to be the Messiah, the true King of the Jews, was in Bethlehem.

Herod called his soldiers to him. He commanded them to go to Bethlehem, and to kill every child there under the age of two. The soldiers set out before sunrise the next morning. Yet the child they sought was already slipping out of their reach, for the night before Joseph had yet another dream.

In this dream, Gabriel, the angel of

the Lord, appeared to Joseph and warned him to flee at once. "Arise! Joseph! Arise!" the angel cried. "Take the baby Jesus and Mary this night and flee with them into Egypt, for Herod even now seeks the child out to destroy him!"

Joseph woke up, and did as the angel commanded. It was a sad journey. Neither Joseph nor Mary wanted to go to Egypt, but longed to remain in their own land, and to go back to their own village of Nazareth. Moreover, they soon heard of

The Flight from Herod

Herod's evil deeds and were filled with grief for the children slaughtered in the town of Bethlehem.

🎵 No one knows where Mary and Joseph and the baby Jesus lived while they were in Egypt, but it is likely that their life there was a hard and humble one. Yet Joseph and Mary managed to keep the child Jesus safe from harm.

🎵 Several years passed, and when Jesus was a young boy, Joseph had another dream. Once again, Gabriel, the angel of

The Story of Christmas

the Lord, appeared before him, only this time Gabriel was smiling. "Joseph!" the angel said. "Listen to me! Awake! Arise! Herod is dead and you may go now and take Jesus back to your home in Nazareth in the land of Israel, where it has been prophesied that he will grow to be wise and strong and good. Go and keep him there, so that he will be called in later days a Nazarene as has been prophesied."

Joseph was glad. He told Mary of the angel's words, and she, too, was full of joy. So they took the boy Jesus back with them to Nazareth.

The Boy Jesus and the First Christmas

So, as the old prophets had foretold, in the village of Nazareth, high in the mountains above the sea of Galilee, the boy Jesus grew. And every year he became stronger in body, and finer and wiser in mind and spirit. The grace of God his Father shone in him brighter each year, preparing him for the day when he would sacrifice himself for his people, and become the King of Kings and lead humankind into his Father's kingdom.

✳ Each year on December 25 we still celebrate Jesus' birthday, and we recall the story of the very first Christmas. We decorate our homes with stars and lights. We put up evergreen trees and boughs of bright holly. We feast and sing songs and we remember the shepherds, and angels, and wise men, and the star, and most of all, Mary, Joseph, and the child in the manger.

The

text of this book was

set in Koch Antiqua with the

display set in Adine Kirnberg Script.

Book design by Maura Fadden Rosenthal

Type set by M Space